Plate 1

Plate 2

Plate 3

Plate 4

Plate 5

Plate 6

Plate 7

Plate 8

To my Valentine

With my Love

I wish I could catch you.

Trust to me.

Constancy.

Bright as these flowers be your life's fair hours.

FOR EVER AYOURS

Hope.

Plate 9

Plate 10

Plate 11

OF ALL THE BOYS I E'ER DID SEE YOU ARE THE ONE MOST DEAR TO ME.

May many friends complete your Joy.

With fond Love.

Your Heart be glad forever.

To the one I love.

A Token of love.

Valentine Greetings

Two Darts with · but · one Heart.

Plate 12

Plate 13

Plate 14

Plate 15

Plate 16

I send love to sing a sweet Valentine Serenade before the window of your heart to which I hope will listen for my sake.

Plate 17

Plate 18

Plate 19

Plate 20

The music of your voice
Just makes my heart rejoice,
For I know that
You are mine,
My own sweet
Valentine.

To my Valentine

Ever faithful.

May hope, thy pilot,
safely steer
Thee thro' all dangers
far or near.

Affection

Plate 21

Plate 22

Plate 23

Plate 24